Logic for Laughs

Higher
Order
Thinking
Skills

Grades 3-6

Written by Melinda E. Clougherty, MS-CCC

ISBN: 0-615-71868-X
ISBN 13: 978-0-615-71868-2

Dedication

I'd like to dedicate this book to my dear friend Pat Sherlock, whose inspiration, creativity and expertise in graphic design has enabled me to publish "Logic for Laughs."

About the Author

Melinda Clougherty is a speech and language pathologist with 29 years of experience working in the public schools. In 2008, she published two guessing games, "Are you in the Doghouse?" and "What's Your Wish?" through School Specialty. In 2011, she published her first book, "Riddled with Riddles," a reproducible classroom activity manual designed to promote critical thinking. Her most recent publication, "Logic for Laughs," was written as a companion book to provide more classroom activities for inferential and deductive reasoning skills.

Introduction

Many generations have been delighted and intrigued by logic puzzles. They enjoy the challenge of solving a mystery or seeking the solution to a problem. Add a twist of humor to these timeless and appealing 'mind games' and the result is a winning combination, "Logic for Laughs." Written by a speech and language pathologist with many years of experience working in the public schools, "Logic for Laughs" will entice even reluctant readers and children with weak inferential and deductive reasoning skills with its entertaining and engaging puzzles!

The use of humor in the classroom to promote critical thinking skills or higher order thinking skills (HOTS) is a prevalent and well respected approach to enhance student learning. Mary Kay Morrison, author of, "Using Humor to Maximize Learning; The Links Between Positive Emotions and Education," who first coined the term 'humergy' (the energy of humor) states: "Humor has the ability to capture the attention of the brain. 'Emotion drives attention and attention drives learning' (Sylvester, 1995). Our brain cannot learn if it is not attending. The surprise elements of humor alert the attentional center of the brain and increase the likelihood of memory storage and long term retrieval. Humor has the potential to hook easily bored and inattentive students. It can help the stressed or shy student to relax. As brain food, humor can't be beat."

- Finding engaging ways to teach HOTS is essential for fulfilling the Common Core Standards which state that students will
- prepare for and participate effectively in a range of conversations and collaborations with diverse partners, building on others' ideas and expressing their own clearly and persuasively.
- read closely to determine what the text says explicitly and to make logical inferences from it.
- cite specific textual evidence when writing or speaking to support conclusions drawn from the text.

The next generation needs to be prepared for a world that requires independent thinkers and problem solvers, not literal thinkers who can only regurgitate factual information.

Versatility is the hallmark of any well-written teacher resource for today's differentiated classroom. "Logic for Laughs" meets this standard with high marks. It can be used

- in a whole class format
- in a small center to provide certain students with extra practice in critical thinking skills
- in competitive teams seeking to solve the puzzle the quickest
- as a 'pair-share'
- to strengthen listening comprehension
- to strengthen reading comprehension
- to supplement the reading curriculum
- for indoor recess
- as a reward

- as a speech and language lesson plan in an inclusive classroom
- as a resource for ESL and Reading teachers

In addition, families will find that these entertaining logic puzzles are perfect for occupying children on rainy days, long car trips, plane trips and birthday parties. Finally, the homeschooling community is always seeking versatile materials that can span the grade three through six age range and provide children with a vigorous opportunity to practice critical thinking skills.

References

Morrison, M.K. (2008) *Using Humor to Maximize Learning: The Links Between Positive Emotions and Education.* Lanham, MD: Rowman and Littlefield Publishing Group, Inc.

Sylvester, R. (1995) *A Celebration of Neurons, an Educator's Guide to the Human Brain.* Alexandria, VA: Association for Supervision and Curriculum Development

HOW TO SOLVE A LOGIC PUZZLE

Got your pencil sharpened? You are about to enter a world of humorous and engaging logic puzzles that are sure to delight your students and entice even the most reluctant ELA students into a set of activities that will strengthen their ability to make important inferences and think deductively and logically.

Most logic puzzles currently on the market involve literal comprehension only. They contain clues such as, "Mary has a blue house but she doesn't live on Maple Ave." It is important to know that the logic puzzles in this book have a totally different flavor to them; they involve inferential and abstract thinking skills. For example, when the reader comes across the clue, "The Reynolds couple named their baby 'Lugnut'," from the six possible answers provided the most likely one is that the Reynolds' favorite hobby is auto racing. Every effort has been made to avoid confusing or overlapping clues.   An answer key is provided at the end of the book as well.

Knowing the strategies involved in solving logic puzzles is also important. One strategy might be to skip over a clue you're not sure about and then come back to it later as more of the pieces of the puzzle fall into place. The second strategy is critical: when an answer has been determined, the corresponding box on the grid is shaded in with your pencil. All boxes in the same row both VERTICALLY and HORIZONTALLY can then be crossed out with X's. Crossing out as many boxes as possible is a strategy that will help your students find all the answers to the puzzle. Also, by crossing out all possible boxes you may end up with five out of six boxes crossed out in a row. When this happens, you can shade in the remaining box as the answer.   This can be done because it is the only possible answer left, i.e., you determined the answer by 'default.'

To help you understand the above, the Halloween Costume Puzzle will be used to illustrate. The story is as follows:

Six children (Jill, Joe, Mary, Penny, John and Bill) go trick-or-treating together every year. This year's costumes are a bat, a princess, a bride, The Hulk, Ironman and a ghost. Read the clues below to find out what each child chose for this year's costume.

Here are your clues:

1. None of the boys would be caught dead wearing a girl's costume.

From this clue, you can cross out all the boys for being a princess or a bride. **Your grid will look like this:**

	bat	princess	bride	The Hulk	Ironman	ghost
Jill						
Joe		X	X			
Mary						
Penny						
John		X	X			
Bill		X	X			

2. None of the girls would be caught dead wearing a boy's costume.

From this clue you can cross out all the girls for being Ironman or The Hulk. **Your grid will now look like this:**

	bat	princess	bride	The Hulk	Ironman	ghost
Jill				X	X	
Joe		X	X			
Mary				X	X	
Penny				X	X	
John		X	X			
Bill		X	X			

3. Joe is not a superhero.

From this clue, you can cross out Joe for being The Hulk or Ironman.
Your grid will now look like this:

	bat	princess	bride	The Hulk	Ironman	ghost
Jill				X	X	
Joe		X	X	X	X	
Mary				X	X	
Penny				X	X	
John		X	X			
Bill		X	X			

4. Neither Mary nor Penny is a princess.

From this clue, you can cross out Mary and Penny for being a
princess. This leaves only one possible person left to be the princess;
it is Jill. Shade in Jill for being the princess and cross out all other
boxes both vertically and horizontally in the same row. *Your grid will
now look like this:*

	bat	princess	bride	The Hulk	Ironman	ghost
Jill	X		X	X	X	X
Joe		X	X	X	X	
Mary		X		X	X	
Penny		X		X	X	
John		X	X			
Bill		X	X			

5. John is bright green.

From this clue, you can shade in John for being The Hulk and cross out all boxes both vertically and horizontally in the same row. This leaves only one possible answer left for Ironman; shade in Bill for being Ironman and cross out all other boxes both vertically and horizontally in the same row. *Your grid will now look like this:*

	bat	princess	bride	The Hulk	Ironman	ghost
Jill	X		X	X	X	X
Joe		X	X	X	X	
Mary		X		X	X	
Penny		X		X	X	
John	X	X	X		X	X
Bill	X	X	X	X		X

6. Mary is dressed in black.

From this clue, you can shade in Mary for being a bat and cross out all other boxes both vertically and horizontally in the same row. This leaves only one possible answer left for the bride. Shade in Penny for being the bride and cross out all the boxes both vertically and horizontally in the same row. This leaves only one possible answer left for the ghost. Shade in Joe for being the ghost. *Your grid will now look like this:*

	bat	princess	bride	The Hulk	Ironman	ghost
Jill	X		X	X	X	X
Joe	X	X	X	X	X	
Mary		X	X	X	X	X
Penny	X	X		X	X	X
John	X	X	X		X	X
Bill	X	X	X	X		X

NOTE: A blank grid is provided in Appendix A to challenge more competent students to set the grid up themselves by reading the text and deciding what information should be on it.

1.

Favorite Game Puzzle

Six children (Billy, Johnny, Mary, Sally, Jimmy and Harry) each have a favorite game: hide and seek, checkers, Go Fish, Candyland, hopscotch and Monopoly. Read the clues below and find out the favorite game for each child.

1) Johnny started playing his favorite game as soon as he learned his colors.

2) Jimmy shares his gameboard with his grandfather who likes to play chess.

3) Billy's favorite game can be played inside or outside.

4) Sally's favorite game can get washed away in the rain.

5) Harry gets mad if he gets sent to jail while playing his favorite game.

6) Mary is very good at shuffling the cards.

	hide and seek	checkers	Go Fish	Candyland	hopscotch	Monopoly
Billy						
Johnny						
Mary						
Sally						
Jimmy						
Harry						

2.

Favorite Shape Puzzle

Six children (Billy, Jimmy, Joey, Sally, Mary and Jane) all have a favorite shape: circle, square, triangle, rectangle, oval and octagon. Read the clues below and find out the favorite shape of each child.

1) Billy's favorite shape makes him think of his new football.

2) Sally's favorite shape has three sides.

3) When Mary and her mother pulled up to a stop sign, she exclaimed, "Look Mom, my favorite shape!"

4) Jane does not like shapes with corners.

5) Jimmy's favorite shape has three syllables.

6) Joey's favorite shape has four equal sides.

	circle	square	triangle	rectangle	oval	octagon
Billy						
Jimmy						
Joey						
Sally						
Mary						
Jane						

3.

Sundae Toppings Puzzle

Mrs. Jenkins told her six children (Cindy, Bill, Sally, Jimmy, Timmy and Sarah) that they could have a bowl of ice cream with one topping: chopped walnuts, hot fudge, chocolate sprinkles, marshmallow fluff, whipped cream or a cherry) if they ate a good dinner. Read the clues below and find out what each child chose for a topping.

1) Bill shook the can before he sprayed his topping on his ice cream.

2) Sally loves the way her topping makes the ice cream melt.

3) Jimmy asked Timmy if he could have his cherry; Timmy said 'no'.

4) Jimmy got a white moustache from his topping.

5) Cindy is afraid to eat chocolate sprinkles; she says they remind her of ants.

6) Sarah enjoys scaring Cindy with her topping.

	chopped walnuts	hot fudge	chocolate sprinkles	marshmallow fluff	whipped cream	cherry
Cindy						
Bill						
Sally						
Jimmy						
Timmy						
Sarah						

4.

Omelettes for Breakfast Puzzle

One morning Farmer Henshaw went out to the henhouse to gather eggs for his family.   His wife was making omelettes for breakfast. Read the clues below and find out what ingredient each family member (Mr. and Mrs. Henshaw, Bill, Jimmy, Joe and Cindy) prefers to have in their omelette: broccoli, spinach, onion, bacon, ham and steak.

1)   None of the boys like green vegetables in their omelette.

2) Both parents and their daughter are vegetarians.

3) Mr. Henshaw likes the same vegetable as Popeye.

4) Mrs. Henshaw's's favorite ingredient has three syllables.

5) Bill's favorite ingredient has one syllable.

6) Joe's favorite ingredient does not come from a pig.

	broccoli	spinach	onion	bacon	ham	steak
Mr. Henshaw						
Mrs. Henshaw						
Bill						
Jimmy						
Joe						
Cindy						

5.

Slumber Party Puzzle

Six girls (Melinda, Ashleigh, Amy, Kayla, Lindsay and Julia) went to a slumber party at Amy's house. One by one, they fell asleep at 9:30 PM, 11:00 PM, 12:00 AM, 12:45 AM and 2:30 AM. Read the clues below to find out when each girl fell asleep.

1) Everyone thought Melinda was a wimp for falling asleep so early.

2) Julia fell asleep an hour after Kayla.

3) Ashleigh got mad when someone put an ice cube down her shirt; she called her mom and went home.

4) At 2:30 AM, Amy's mom came up and yelled, "Lindsay! Stop brake dancing and go to sleep!"

	9:30 PM	11:00 PM	12:00 AM	12:45 AM	2:30 AM	none
Melinda						
Ashleigh						
Amy						
Kayla						
Lindsay						
Julia						

6.

Burping Contest Puzzle

Six brothers (Joe, Billy, Harry, Steve, John and Jake) were bored one day so they decided to enter the burping contest down at the local Moose Club Lodge. The timer was set for five minutes and whoever burped the most would win a case of Moosehead root beer. Read the clues below to find out how each brother performed in the contest; 0 burps, 1 burp, 5 burps, 9 burps, 10 burps and 18 burps.

1) Joe's girlfriend broke up with him after he won the contest.

2) Billy is so polite, he couldn't burp at all; he still got a free t-shirt for trying.

3) Steve only burped once, but he got a free t-shirt for being the loudest.

4) Harry guzzled a soda and managed to produce one more burp than John.

5) Jake burped half as many times as Harry.

	0 burps	1 burp	5 burps	9 burps	10 burps	18 burps
Joe						
Billy						
Harry						
Steve						
John						
Jake						

7.

Babysitter in Tears Puzzle

Mr. and Mrs. Henry went out to dinner and left their six children (Davie, Wendy, Jenny, Jimmy, Shelly and Tommy) with a new babysitter. When they came home a couple of hours later the house was a disaster area and the babysitter was sitting in a puddle of tears. Read the clues below and find out what each child did to misbehave: climbed up the chimney, put a newspaper in the dryer, shaved the cat, put salt in the sugar bowl, decorated the dog with holiday lights and hid the babysitter's cell phone.

1) The babysitter had to give Davie a bath after he misbehaved.

2) The babysitter had to call the fire department after Wendy misbehaved.

3) Jimmy took something that didn't belong to him.

4) Shelly offered to make the babysitter a nice hot cup of tea.

5) The cat was not shaved by a girl.

	climbed up the chimney	put a newspaper In the dryer	shaved the cat	put salt in the sugar bowl	decorated the dog	hid the babysitter's cell phone
Davie						
Wendy						
Jenny						
Jimmy						
Shelly						
Tommy						

8.

Shirley's Blind Dates Puzzle #1

Shirley Brissette joined a dating service and was delighted when she was invited out on six blind dates on six consecutive nights, beginning on a Sunday. Read the clues below and find out which night she went out with each date (John, Joe, Bill, Harry, Neal, Steve).

1) She went out with the two men whose first initial is 'J' in alphabetical order on Sunday and Monday.

2) She enjoyed her Friday night date with Bill the most.

3) She went out with Neal two days after Harry.

	John	Joe	Bill	Harry	Neal	Steve
Sunday						
Monday						
Tuesday						
Wednesday						
Thursday						
Friday						

9.

Shirley's Blind Dates Puzzle #2

Shirley Brissette is a popular girl who likes to go out on dates but lately she has not enjoyed herself. Each time she went out this week, the guy had a flaw in his personality (boring, conceited, klutzy, cheap, rude and always late). Read the clues below and find out why Shirley had a lousy time with: Bill, Phil, Lanndon, Nathan, Edward and Jeffrey.

1) On her first date with Jeffrey, he bought her peanut butter crackers and a ginger ale and sat in the parking lot.

2) On their first date, Edward asked, "When are you going to do something about that nose of yours?"

3) On their first date, Nathan had to take Shirley to the emergency room after he accidentally dropped a bowling ball on her toes.

4) On his date, Lanndon insisted on talking about his toothpick collection all night.

5) Bill showed up at 7:30 PM for a 6:00 PM date. He had a nice car so she went out with him anyway.

6) On his date Phil said, "You're the third pretty girl I've gone out with this week."

	boring	conceited	klutzy	cheap	rude	always late
Bill						
Phil						
Lanndon						
Nathan						
Edward						
Jeffrey						

10.

Shirley's Blind Dates Puzzle #3

Shirley Brissette is a very charming and popular girl who enjoys going out on dates with a variety of interesting men. This week she was invited out for dinner every night from Sunday through Friday by men with the following professions: goalie, pitcher, waiter, chef, fire fighter, and life guard. Read the clues below to find out the profession of Shirley's date each night.

1) Shirley did not date any men who rescue people on Monday, Wednesday or Friday.

2) She did not date an athlete on Sunday, Tuesday or Thursday.

3) No one from the food industry dated Shirley on Monday, Wednesday or Thursday.

4) She did not date any profession that ends with 'er' on Sunday or Tuesday.

5) She did not date the goalie on Monday.

6) She dated the chef first.

	goalie	pitcher	waiter	chef	firefighter	lifeguard
Sunday						
Monday						
Tuesday						
Wednesday						
Thursday						
Friday						

11.

Diet Contest Puzzle

Six friends (Betty, Judy, Phyllis, Sylvia, Jennifer and Alyssa) decided to go on a diet together for two months. Then they had a little party to weigh themselves and the following results were found; lost 3 lbs, lost 4 lbs, lost 8 lbs, lost 11 lbs, lost 15 lbs and gained 5 lbs. Read the clues below to find out what the results were for each friend.

1) Betty lost twice as much weight as Judy.

2) Phyllis loves doughnuts so she lost the least weight.

3) Sylvia cried when she stepped on the scale.

4) Jennifer was pleased that she lost more weight than her best friend, Alyssa.

	lost 3 lbs.	lost 4 lbs.	lost 8 lbs.	lost 11 lbs.	lost 15 lbs.	gained 5 lbs.
Betty						
Judy						
Phyllis						
Sylvia						
Jennifer						
Alyssa						

12.

Hotdog Eating Contest Puzzle

Six brothers (John, Joe, George, Bill, Harry and Sam) decided to enter a hotdog eating contest. The following number of hotdogs was consumed: 3, 7, 12, 13, 14, and 18. Read the clues below to find out how each brother performed in the contest.

1) John ate the most hotdogs and then was taken away on a stretcher.

2) Joe did not eat an even number of hotdogs.

3) George did eat an even number of hotdogs.

4) Bill was disqualified when he tried to slip his fourth hotdog to his dachshund under the table.

5) Harry ate two less hotdogs than George.

6) Sam ate an unlucky number of hotdogs.

	3 hot dots	7 hot dogs	12 hot dogs	13 hot dogs	14 hot dogs	18 hot dogs
John						
Joe						
George						
Bill						
Harry						
Sam						

13.

Restaurant Puzzle

Six friends went out to dinner together (Joe, Virginia, Melissa, Bill, John and Susan). They each ordered something different: spaghetti and meatballs, small salad, eggplant parmesan, burger and fries, baked haddock, and clam chowder. Read the clues to find out what each friend ordered.

1) When Joe tried to stab his dinner with a fork, it rolled off the plate and onto the floor.

2) Virginia is a vegetarian.

3) Melissa is on a diet.

4) Bill asked Susan if he could have one of her French fries.

5) John ate his dinner with a spoon.

	spaghetti and meatballs	small salad	eggplant parmesan	burger and fries	baked haddock	clam chowder
Joe						
Virginia						
Melissa						
Bill						
John						
Susan						

14.

Disasters Puzzle

Six friends (Todd, Jill, Bill, Mary, John and Fred) went to their college reunion and were surprised to find out that they had all experienced some kind of a disaster in the last year: fire, flood, tornado, earthquake, hurricane and blizzard. Read the clues below to find out which disaster each person experienced.

1) When his disaster was over, Todd said, "Toto, I don't think we're in Kansas anymore."

2) After her disaster ended, Jill spent the morning digging out her mailbox.

3) Bill's disaster was caused by his neighbor's careless smoking.

4) Mary's disaster was named 'Betty' because it was the second one of the season.

5) John woke up in the middle of the night and shouted, "Why did I move to San Francisco?"

6) Fred and his dog, Rufus paddled their way to safety in a bathtub.

	fire	flood	tornado	earthquake	hurricane	blizzard
Todd						
Jill						
Bill						
Mary						
John						
Fred						

15.

Psychic Puzzle

Six friends (Sue, Mary, Jill, Penny, Cathy, and Nancy) decided to throw a party and invite a psychic for entertainment. Read the clues below to find out what the psychic told each friend about her future: marry four husbands, find the cure for bad breath, solve the global warming problem, invent the perfect potato masher, develop a pill that promotes weight loss and be abducted by aliens.

1) Mary was not told that she would help mankind.

2) Sue was told that she would put Weight Watchers out of business.

3) Jill was told that she would be given an award from the Idaho Potato Farmers Guild.

4) Penny was told that she would save the world from the brink of destruction.

5) Cathy was told that nobody would believe her story.

6) Nancy was told that people would thank her for her contribution to the world.

	marry four husbands	find cure for bad breath	solve the global warming problem	invent the perfect potato masher	develop a pill that promotes weight loss	abducted by aliens
Sue						
Mary						
Jill						
Penny						
Cathy						
Nancy						

16.

Food Fight Puzzle

One night six children in the Henderson family (Jeremy, Jill, Jenny, Mary, Ethan and Baby Tom) got into a food fight. They made a huge mess using the following foods: ketchup, grapes, doughnuts, whipped cream, baby food and banana cream pie. Read the clues below to find out which food each child used as a weapon.

1) Jeremy squeezed a bottle upside down over his brother's head.

2) When Jill threw some food, Jenny caught one in her mouth.

3) Mary shook something really well before she sprayed her brother in the face with it.

4) Jenny twirled something on her finger and then chucked it at her brother.

5) Even the eight-month-old was able to participate in his own way.

6) Ethan threw something that had a crust.

	baby food	whipped cream	grapes	banana cream pie	doughnuts	ketchup
Jeremy						
Jill						
Jenny						
Mary						
Ethan						
Baby Tom						

17.

School Nurse Puzzle

Six children (Bill, Mary, Joe, Jill, Johnny and Sue) were sent to see the school nurse at the Willett School. They each had a different problem: head lice, homesick, splinter, headache, fell in a puddle and difficulty hearing. Read the clues below to find out why each child was sent to visit Mrs. Ryan in her nurse's office.

1) Bill says, "Huh?" a lot.

2) Mary's problem was embarrassing and itchy.

3) Joe needed a change of clothes.

4) Jill's problem was above her neck.

5) Johnny's problem required tweezers.

6) Sue's problem was solved with a hug.

	head lice	homesick	splinter	headache	fell in a puddle	difficulty hearing
Bill						
Mary						
Joe						
Jill						
Johnny						
Sue						

18.

Halloween Costume Puzzle

Six children (Jill, Joe, Mary, Penny, John and Bill) go trick-or-treating together every year. This year's costumes are a bat, a princess, a bride, The Hulk, Ironman, and a ghost. Read the clues below to find out what each child chose for this year's costume.

1) None of the boys would be caught dead wearing a girl's costume.

2) None of the girls would be caught dead wearing a boy's costume.

3) Joe is not a superhero.

4) Neither Mary nor Penny is a princess.

5) John is bright green.

6) Mary is dressed in black.

	bat	princess	bride	The Hulk	Ironman	ghost
Jill						
Joe						
Mary						
Penny						
John						
Bill						

19.

Commuting to Work Puzzle

Six friends (Carl, Justin, Tex, Luke, Ahmed and Nathan) all commute to work in a different way: train, horse, car, camel, limousine and on foot. Read the clues below to find out how each friend gets to work each morning.

1) Luke enjoys chatting with his chauffeur on the way to work.

2) Carl is able to read the newspaper on his way to work.

3) Tex stopped to buy some carrots for his trusted Palomino on his way to work.

4) Justin used his gasoline credit card on his way to work.

5) Ahmed likes to stop for a drink of water at an oasis on his way to work.

6) Nathan got mugged twice on his way to work this week.

	train	horse	car	camel	limousine	on foot
Carl						
Justin						
Tex						
Luke						
Ahmed						
Nathan						

20.

Treats at Circus Puzzle

Six children in the Shaw family (Bill, Sally, Mary, Tony, Benjamin and George) were taken to the circus one weekend. Their parents gave them each enough money to buy something at the concession stand: stuffed animal, t-shirt, wax lips, peanuts, and cotton cand). Read the clues below and find out what each child bought at the circus.

1)   Benjamin wanted to look like the funny clown he saw in the performance.

2) Sally bought something to cuddle with in bed.

3) The twins, Mary and Tony bought the same thing only Mary's was pink and Tony's was blue.

4) Bill wore his souvenir to school the following week.

5) George shared his treat with the elephants.

	stuffed animal	t-shirt	wax lips	peanuts	pink cotton candy	blue cotton candy
Billy						
Sally						
Mary						
Tony						
Benjamin						
George						

21.

Dog Tricks Puzzle

The Griffin family owns six dogs (Ralph, Topper, Boomer, Bailey, Skittles and T-bone) who all have a special talent: fold the laundry, guess your age, mow the lawn, sell lemonade, knit a sweater, play volleyball. Read the clues below and find out the special talent of each pooch.

1) Ralph's team has won the tournament for two years in a row.

2) Boomer donates his profits to charity.

3) Topper's family goes to the movies wearing matching cardigans.

4) Bailey takes the winter off.

5) Skittles is hardly ever wrong.

6) When T-Bone is done with his chore, he likes to curl up in the basket for a cozy nap.

	mow the lawn	sell lemonade	knit a sweater	guess your age	play volleyball	fold the laundry
Ralph						
Topper						
Boomer						
Bailey						
Skittles						
T-bone						

22.

Unusual Hair Color Puzzle

Deborah is a teenager who loves to drive her parents crazy by dyeing her hair a different color every day. Her friends admire her new hair color every morning and try their best to think of a matching nickname. Read the clues below and find out the color of Deborah's hair on each day of the week, starting with Monday (black and white, purple, red, brown, hot pink, and green).

1) On Tuesday, they named her 'Seaweed.'

2) On Wednesday, they named her 'Zebra.'

3) On Monday, they named her 'Highlighter.'

4) On Thursday, they named her 'Mud Pie.'

5) On Friday, they named her 'Ketchup.'

6) On Saturday, they named her 'Eggplant.'

	black and white	purple	red	brown	hot pink	green
Monday						
Tuesday						
Wednesday						
Thursday						
Friday						
Saturday						

23.

Unusual Diet Puzzle

Harold has very odd eating habits. From Monday through Saturday every week, he only eats one kind of food (bananas, cotton candy, salad, popcorn, milk shakes and peanuts) all day long. Read the clues below and find out which food he eats each day.

1) Harold has to make sure that his blender is working on Thursdays.

2) Harold feels like swinging from limb to limb on Mondays.

3) Harold always has sticky fingers on Fridays.

4) Harold likes to pretend he is an elephant on the weekend.

5) Harold likes to diet on Tuesdays.

6) Harold likes to go to the movies every Wednesday.

	bananas	cotton candy	salad	popcorn	milk shake	peanuts
Monday						
Tuesday						
Wednesday						
Thursday						
Friday						
Saturday						

24.

Places to Sleep Puzzle

One night Mrs. Reynolds came home late after work. Her husband had already gone to bed. She quickly checked on her children (Tommy, Ginny, Sally, Johnny, Billy and Melissa) to make sure they were all safely asleep where they belong: sleeping bag, cot, cradle, hotel, couch and bunk bed. Read the clues below to find out where each child is sleeping.

1) Billy climbed a ladder, snuggled up with his teddy bear and was soon snoring softly.

2) The teenager, Johnny fell asleep in the rumpus room with his clothes on.

3) Ginny always falls asleep quickly if you rock her back and forth gently.

4) Tommy built a fort using a blanket and a card table. Dad let him make a bed underneath and sleep there.

5) Sally shares a small bedroom with her sister. In the morning, she folds up her bed and puts it back in the closet.

6) Melissa wasn't home tonight because she got invited to Disney World with her friend's family.

	sleeping bag	cot	cradle	hotel	couch	bunk bed
Tommy						
Ginny						
Sally						
Johnny						
Billy						
Melissa						

25.

The Horse's Birthday Puzzle

Mindy bought her horse Mariah, twenty- two years ago. Each year Mindy celebrates the horse's birthday by baking a cake made from bran mash, carrots and apples. This is always followed by a series of presents.   Read the clues below and find out the order in which this gray Arabian mare opens her presents (saddle, bridle, bucket, blanket, trailer and carrots).

1)   The first present the horse opened made a loud crunching sound.

2) The second present kept her warm in the winter.

3) Her third present made sure she was never thirsty.

4) Her fourth present was something she could wear on her back.

5) She wore her fifth present to her next horse show.

6) Her sixth present was the most expensive of all.

	saddle	bridle	bucket	blanket	trailer	carrots
First present						
Second present						
Third Present						
Fourth present						
Fifth present						
Sixth present						

26.

Emotions Puzzle

The Doherty family (Mr. Doherty, Jill, Steve, George, Jessica, Alyssa) all have different experiences one week. Read the clues below and find out the emotion they felt as a result: lazy, angry, proud, embarrassed, starving and jealous.

1) Jill forgot to dressed one morning and showed up in school wearing pajamas.

2) Steve went to the state championship and won first prize for spelling the word 'onomatopoeia' correctly.

3) George hiked across three mountain ranges in New Hampshire carrying nothing but a canteen of water and a granola bar.

4) Jessica flew to the Bahamas for a week's vacation and sat on the beach sipping lemonade.

5) Mr. Doherty went shopping at the mall and when he returned to his car he found a large dent in its side.

6) Alyssa went on a job interview at the same company as her best friend who ended up being offered the job.

	lazy	angry	proud	embarrassed	starving	jealous
Mr. Doherty						
Jill						
Steve						
George						
Jessica						
Alyssa						

27.

Stuffed Animals on the Bed Puzzle

Benjamin has six favorite stuffed animals (kangaroo, anteater, camel, turtle, raccoon and iguana). Every morning he makes his bed and arranges them in a different order on the pillow. Read the clues below to find out what order Benjamin put his stuffed animals this morning.

1) The first animal has a weird diet.

2) The second animal can live in a harsh habitat.

3) The third animal looks like a mini dinosaur.

4) The fourth animal cannot usually win a race.

5) The fifth animal looks like a bandit.

6) The sixth animal has a special storage compartment.

	kangaroo	anteater	camel	turtle	raccoon	iguana
First						
Second						
Third						
Fourth						
Fifth						
Sixth						

28.

A Rainy Day Puzzle

Six children (Billy, Jane, John, Mary, Little Joey, Jennifer) had to find something to do on a rainy Saturday. Read the clues below to find out how each child kept themselves occupied: pretend play, draw, jump rope, hide and seek, bake cookies, write poetry. Read the clues below to find out what each child did on a rainy day.

1)   Billy and his play date had a sword fight.

2) Mary made the house smell heavenly.

3) Little Joey won a game by spending hours in a closet.

4) Jennifer asked, "What rhymes with Cincinnati?"

5) John spent the day sketching superheroes.

6) Jane went out on the porch to get some exercise.

	pretend play	draw	jump rope	hide and seek	bake cookies	write poetry
Billy						
Jane						
John						
Mary						
Little Joey						
Jennifer						

29.

Favorite Food Puzzle

Six children in the Marino family (Stephanie, Marta, Lanndon, Melissa, Christopher and Sarah) all have a favorite food: brownies, cotton candy, French fries, hot dogs, watermelon and pancakes. Read the clues below to find each child's favorite food.

1) Christopher's favorite food makes him more cheerful in the morning.

2) Marta's likes to put walnuts in her favorite food.

3) Lanndon prefers to cook his favorite food on the grill.

4) Stephanie enjoys spitting the seeds of her favorite food at her brother.

5) Melissa's favorite food is usually pink or blue.

6) Sarah won't eat her favorite food without ketchup.

	brownies	cotton candy	French fries	hot dog	watermelon	pancakes
Stephanie						
Marta						
Lanndon						
Melissa						
Christopher						
Sarah						

30.

Stargazing Puzzle

Six children in the Brennan family (Mae, Sarah, Travis, Lucy, Noah,and Eric) all looked through a telescope in the back yard one night and each saw something different: an alien, the Milky Way, a cloud, a comet, the Big Dipper and Saturn. Read the clues below to find out what each child saw in the night sky.

1) Mae saw something that had the name of a candy bar.

2) Noah saw something made of ice and dust.

3) Sarah saw something that was shaped like a soup ladle.

4) Travis didn't see much at all.

5) Eric saw something that had rings.

6) Lucy screamed and ran in the house after she looked through the telescope.

	alien	Milky Way	cloud	comet	Big Dipper	Saturn
Mae						
Sarah						
Travis						
Lucy						
Noah						
Eric						

31.

Favorite Sounds Puzzle

Six friends at school (Abigail, James, Jennifer, Amanda, William and Jonathan) went out to recess and talked about their favorite sound: rumbling, sizzling, creaking, crackling, squealing, and purring. Read the clues below to find out the sound that each child enjoys hearing.

1) Jennifer loves to build a bonfire.

2) Jonathan loves a good thunderstorm.

3) James wandered into a haunted house

4) Amanda loves to have bacon for breakfast.

5) William grew up on a pig farm.

6) Abigail loves her new kitten.

	rumbling	sizzling	creaking	crackling	squealing	purring
Abigail						
James						
Jennifer						
Amanda						
William						
Jonathan						

32.

Hide and Seek Puzzle

Six children in the Pendleton family (Peter, James, Marisa, Linda, William and Susie) decided to play hide and seek on a rainy day. Their hiding places were: behind the living room couch, under the bed, on the back porch, in the fireplace, in the dog's crate and in the chandelier. Read the clues below to find out where each child hid.

   1)   Susie had to make sure that the curtains didn't move.

   2) Linda got a little sooty in her hiding place.

   3) Marisa was grounded for ruining the ceiling.

   4) William pretended to bark when he was found.

   5) Peter spent his time counting the shoes until he was found.

   6) James got a little chilly waiting to be found.

	behind the living room couch	under the bed	on the back porch	in the fireplace	in the dog's crate	in the chandelier
Peter						
James						
Marisa						
Linda						
William						
Susie						

33.

Good Samaritan Puzzle

Six children in the Farinella family (Jerry, Bill, Jill, Jessica, Dan and Belinda) believe in helping their neighbors in need. They help out by: shoveling the snow, running a charity car wash, working at an animal shelter, driving a neighbor to an appointment, raking the leaves and rescuing the cat from a tree. Read the clues below to find out each child contributes towards other people's needs.

1) Jill is the only one old enough to have a driver's license.

2) Bill helps out his neighbors in the wintertime.

3) Dan convinced his mother to give a puppy a good home.

4) Jessica and her cheerleader friends came home from their volunteer work soaking wet, sunburned and happy.

5) Belinda needed a ladder to perform her act of charity.

6) Jerry sometimes gets a blister on his thumb.

	shovel snow	run a charity car wash	work at an animal shelter	drive a neighbor to an appointment	rake leaves	rescue a cat from a tree
Jerry						
Bill						
Jill						
Jessica						
Dan						
Belinda						

34.

Bad Boss Puzzle

All of the employees at the Super Duper Bubble Gum Company (secretary, shipping department, limousine driver, salesman, custodian and accountant) are in a good mood this week because the boss is away on a business trip. However, each day, beginning on a Monday, the boss calls and leaves one of them a nasty message on the voice mail. Read the clues below to find out who the boss yells at each day.

1) On Monday, the boss called and shouted, "Catherine, call the florist and have them send some flowers to my second wife. She's mad at me for being away so much."

2) On Tuesday, he left a message, "Peter, if that package doesn't go out on time, heads are going to roll!"

3) On Wednesday, he called to inquire, "Laura, can I deduct child support payments on my income tax return? My ex-wife is costing me a fortune!"

4) On Thursday, he called and yelled, "Jim if those sales figures don't improve this month, I'm demoting you to the mail room!"

5) On Friday, he called and screamed, "John, don't forget to put some rat poison down in the warehouse."

6) On Saturday he called and warned, "Pedro, if I have to wait even two minutes to be picked up at the airport, I'll have your head on a platter!"

	secretary	shipping department	limousine driver	salesman	custodian	accountant
Monday						
Tuesday						
Wednesday						
Thursday						
Friday						
Saturday						

35.

What a Nightmare Puzzle

Each night Mr. and Mrs. Jefferson go to bed around 10:00 PM. Mr. Jefferson suffers from nightmares. Each morning when he wakes up, he asks his wife what he was yelling about in his sleep and she tells him. His nightmares include: threatened by a growling dog, swept up by a tornado, died, got lost in a strange city, inherited a skunk farm, and drowned in maple syrup. Read the clues below and figure out what nightmare he had each night, beginning on a Monday.

1) On Monday night he kept grumbling, "Where's the goddamned map when you need one?"

2) On Tuesday night he mumbled, "Nice doggie, good poochie."

3) On Wednesday night, he yelled, "Quick, someone throw me a pancake!"

4) On Thursday night he commented, "Toto, I don't think we're in Kansas anymore."

5) On Friday night he stated, "No, the cheaper casket will be just fine.

6) On Saturday night he exclaimed, "Peeeeeee-you!"

	threatened by a growling dog	swept up by a tornado	died	got lost in a strange city	inherited a skunk farm	drowned in maple syrup
Monday						
Tuesday						
Wednesday						
Thursday						
Friday						
Saturday						

36.

Life of Crime Puzzle

Six friends (George, Sam, Bob, Owen, Nathan and Phil) grew up together in a small town. Coincidentally, when they became adults, they all pursued a life of crime, got arrested in the same month, and were sentenced and sent to the same jail. Read the clues below to find out the crime that each old friend committed: shoplifting, grand theft auto, forgery, bank robbery, illegal gambling and counterfeiting.

1)   Sam owns an expensive set of fountain pens.

2)   Bob was driven to jail by his bookie.

3)   Phil got the shortest sentence.

4)   Owen tried to buy bubble gum with Monopoly money when he was a kid.

5)   George was arrested in the mall parking lot.

6)   Nathan plans on buying a tropical island when he gets out of jail.

	shoplifting	grand theft auto	forgery	bank robbery	illegal gambling	counterfeiting
George						
Sam						
Bob						
Owen						
Nathan						
Phil						

37.

Accident Prone Son Puzzle

Poor Mrs. Stewart! Her son, Dennis is very accident prone. She finds herself visiting the emergency room at least once a week. This week has been the worse one ever! Dennis injured himself every day in a row, beginning on a Monday. Read the clues below and figure out what happened to Dennis (poisoning, concussion, poison ivy, black eye, burnt eyelashes and fell off a cliff).

1) On Monday, Dennis' mother wished she had never let him toast a marshmallow at the Boy Scout cook-out.

2) Come to think of it, letting him try his hand at Pin the Tail on the Donkey on Tuesday wasn't such a hot idea either.

3) Similarly, skateboarding at the park on Wednesday also did not go very well for Dennis.

4) On Thursday, Dennis told a boy in his class, "You run like a girl." He lived to regret it.

5) Dennis' soccer ball got kicked into the woods on Friday. He went to retrieve it…

6) On Saturday, Dennis ate some funny looking mushrooms in his backyard.

	poisoning	concussion	poison ivy	black eye	burnt eyelashes	fell off a cliff
Monday						
Tuesday						
Wednesday						
Thursday						
Friday						
Saturday						

38.

Mixed Up Suitcases Puzzle

Six people (a psychic, a beauty queen, a body builder, a jeweler, a hippie and a snake charmer) all got on a plane to Las Vegas. They each had a plain black suitcase. When they landed, things got a little hectic at the baggage claim area. Unfortunately, none of them retrieved the correct suitcase. When they got to their hotel, they opened the suitcase and realized their mistake. Read the clues below and help them identify the correct owner of each suitcase.

1) When the psychic opened her suitcase, she was astounded to find a sleeping boa constrictor.

2) When the jeweler opened his suitcase, all he found were a bunch of tie-dyed t-shirts.

3) When the snake charmer opened his suitcase, he found some tarot cards and a crystal ball.

4) When the body builder opened his suitcase, he found an evening gown and a pair of high heels.

5) When the hippie opened his suitcase, he found diamonds, rubies and sapphires.

6) When the beauty queen opened her suitcase, she found a set of heavy barbells.

	psychic's suitcase	beauty queen's suitcase	body builder's suitcase	jeweler's suitcase	hippie's suitcase	snake charmer's suitcase
Psychic						
Beauty queen						
Body builder						
Jeweler						
Hippie						
Snake charmer						

39.

The Car That was a Lemon Puzzle

Brad saved up all his money for six months and proudly bought himself a shiny new convertible. Boy oh boy, what a lemon it turned out to be! Each day something else on the car failed to work properly (broken speedometer, flat tire, broken windshield wiper, muffler fell off, broken horn and a hole in the gas tank). Beginning on a Monday, read the clues below to find out what problem Brad had with his car each day.

1) On Monday, Brad was driving along when he heard a loud crash. He looked in his rearview mirror and saw a large tailpipe lying in the road.

2) On Tuesday, Brad got stranded along the side of the road. Luckily someone came along with a jack to help him.

3) On Wednesday, he pumped $50 worth of gas into the car. He drove only 10 miles and the needle on the gas tank was down to 'empty.'

4) On Thursday, he had a very difficult time seeing the road in the rain.

5) On Friday, he tried to honk at a squirrel at the side of the road and nothing happened.

6) On Saturday, he got pulled over for speeding.

	broken speedometer	flat tire	broken windshield wiper	muffler fell off	broken horn	hole in the gas tank
Monday						
Tuesday						
Wednesday						
Thursday						
Friday						
Saturday						

40.

The Very Rude Daughter Puzzle #1

Mrs. Brown had a very beautiful daughter named Lynette whom many men were interested in dating. However, Lynette was so rude to them, they usually never called back to ask for a second date. Read the clues below to find out what insulting comment Lynette made on each date: his crooked teeth, the car he drove, his weight, his baldness, his clothes or his education).

1) When Brandon came to pick her up Lynette exclaimed, "You don't expect me to die in this old rust bucket, do you?"

2) Gregory brought Lynette to a restaurant with a pub menu. She told him, "You don't want to order those nachos. They are way too fattening."

3) Lynette went out with Matthew to a Chinese food restaurant. After they ordered their food she asked, "So, when did you first start losing your hair?"

4) The next night Lynette went out with Rob. They got as far as dessert when she calmly asked, "Couldn't your family afford braces?"

5) Lynette's next date was with Adam. They ordered some hot wings for an appetizer. By the time their entrees came she inquired, "Where did you go to college? Your vocabulary and grammar are atrocious!"

6) Lynette's latest date was with Christopher. He got as far as the front door when she sputtered, "Where did you get that suit, the Salvation Army?"

	his crooked teeth	the car he drove	his weight	his baldness	his clothes	his education
Brandon						
Gregory						
Matthew						
Rob						
Adam						
Christopher						

41.

Very Rude Daughter Puzzle #2

Mrs. Brown had a very beautiful daughter named Lynette whom many men were interested in dating. However, Lynette was so rude to them, they usually never called back to ask for a second date. Read the clues below to find out what insulting comment Lynette made on each date: his cologne, his class ring, his buck teeth, his physique, his IQ and his tie.

1) When Lynette went out to dinner with Charles she advised him, "You should join a gym. You'd get more dates."

2) When Lynette went to a poetry reading with Jim she snarled, "Did you get in the wrong line when they were giving out brains?"

3) On her date with Phil she exclaimed, "Yuck! What died in here?"

4) During dinner with Ben she inquired, "Did you buy that in a gumball machine?"

5) At an Italian restaurant with Sergio she asked, "Who dressed you this morning, Sponge Bob Square Pants?"

6) At a Chinese restaurant with George she inquired, "Are you descended from beavers?"

	his cologne	his class ring	his buck teeth	his physique	his IQ	his tie
Charles						
Jim						
Phil						
Ben						
Sergio						
George						

42.

Very Rude Daughter Puzzle #3

Mrs. Brown had a very beautiful daughter named Lynette whom many men were interested in dating. However, Lynette was so rude to them, they usually never called back to ask for a second date. Read the clues below to find out what insulting comment Lynette made on each date: his condo, his nose, his ears, his short stature, his yellow teeth, his conversational skills.

1) On her date with Nathan she suggested, "Why don't we ask the waitress to bring you a booster seat."

2) At a bistro with Jack she suggested, "You should wear a yellow tie so it matches your smile."

3) When Lynette went out with Jeremy she asked, "Have you ever seen a movie called 'Dumbo'?"

4) On her date with Lennie she observed, "You're not that bad-looking until you turn your head sideways."

5) At a steakhouse with Mario she pretended to fall asleep in her soup.

6) When Sam brought her back to his place after dinner she asked, "Was this place a foreclosure?"

	his condo	his nose	his ears	his short stature	his yellow teeth	his conversational skills
Nathan						
Jack						
Jeremy						
Lennie						
Mario						
Sam						

43.

Very Rude Daughter Puzzle #4

Mrs. Brown had a very beautiful daughter named Lynette whom many men were interested in dating. However, Lynette was so rude to them, they usually never called back to ask for a second date. Read the clues below to find out what insulting comment Lynette made on each date: his looks, his table manners, his paunch, his cell phone, his artwork and his double chin.

1) On her date with Bart she inquired, "Is it hard for you to bend over to tie your shoes?"

2) At a pub with Sam she requested, "Could you ask the waitress to turn the lights down lower?"

3) On her date with Jeremy she asked, "Does your mother still cut your meat for you?"

4) When Lynette went out with Jack she asked, "Did you buy that in a gumball machine?"

5) When Steve brought her back to his place after dinner she asked, "Did you paint this by number?"

6) On her date with Bill she stated, "If you eat that, you'll grow a third one."

	his looks	his table manners	his paunch	his cell phone	his artwork	his double chin
Bart						
Sam						
Jeremy						
Jack						
Steve						
Bill						

44.

Little Billy's Revenge Puzzle

One night Mr. and Mrs. Chisholm went out to dinner. They left their older teenage children (Olivia, Mark, Lauren, Peter, Ben and Robin) in charge of baby-sitting three-year-old Billy. Billy wanted to stay up late to watch a movie with the older kids but they made him go to bed at 7:00 PM. He was so mad he decided to put something in each of his sibling's shoes to get revenge. Read the clues below to find out what Billy put in each person's shoe: potato chips, super glue, frog, toothpaste, pebble and thimble.

1) When Olivia found something in her shoe she thought, "How strange." She put it back in her mother's sewing kit.

2) When Mark took his shoe off after school that day, his sock came off, too.

3) When Lauren put her shoe on, she heard a crunching sound.

4) When Peter went to school the next day he wondered, "What smells so minty?"

5) When Ben put his shoe on, he had to take it off again and shake it out.

6) Robin tried to put her shoe on but something kept croaking inside. She screamed and ran to get her mother.

	potato chips	super glue	frog	toothpaste	pebble	thimble
Olivia						
Mark						
Lauren						
Peter						
Ben						
Robin						

45.

Todd's Aliens Puzzle

One night Todd woke up at 2:00 AM to find three aliens staring at him from the foot of the bed. "Will you help us?" they asked, "Our queen sent us here to bring back an invention from Earth." Todd agreed to help them and they went home happy. Every month the aliens returned and Todd sent them home with something new for the queen. Read the clues below and find out what Todd gave to the aliens from January through June (hair elastics, a ladder, a mirror, a thimble, a puppy and an air conditioner).

1)   In January, the aliens came and told Todd that the queen was complaining about global warming on their planet.

2) In February, the aliens came and told Todd that the queen had taken up quilting.

3)   In March, the aliens came back to visit and told Todd that the queen wants to know what she looks like.

4) In April, when the aliens visited they said, "The queen wants her palace to be painted."

5) In May, the aliens came to say that the queen was feeling lonely.

6) In June, the aliens came to say that the queen wants to try her hair in braids.

	hair elastics	ladder	mirror	thimble	puppy	air conditioner
January						
February						
March						
April						
May						
June						

46.

Joe's Exotic Careers Puzzle

Joe was a man of many talents who had six highly unusual careers in his lifetime. Each career was somewhat dangerous so he didn't dare to do any one of them for very long. Read the clues below and find out the order in which Joe practiced each career: trapeze artist, sumo wrestler, alligator wrestler, snake charmer, sword swallower and dolphin trainer.

1) Joe had to give up his first career when he discovered that his wet suit kept giving him a rash.

2) He gave up his second career when he didn't weigh enough to compete.

3) Joe's third career didn't work out because he was afraid of heights.

4) He kept getting bitten for his fourth career so that one ended, too.

5) Joe's fifth career gave him a terrible sore throat.

6) He gave up his last career when his wife told him he had to choose between the boa constrictor and her.

	trapeze artist	sumo wrestler	alligator wrestler	snake charmer	sword swallower	dolphin trainer
First career						
Second career						
Third career						
Fourth career						
Fifth career						
Sixth career						

47.

Unusual Weddings Puzzle #1

Six couples (Henderson, Madden, Simon, Shaw, Willard and Traut) got married one weekend. They each based their wedding and reception on a theme that represented their profession: sailor, undertaker, jockey, sanitation worker, audiologist and burglar. Read the clues below to find out the theme of each couple's wedding.

1) The Henderson couple got married on horseback.

2) The Madden couple got married at the town dump.

3) The Simon couple broke into an empty mansion for their ceremony.

4) The Shaw couple got married in a sound-proof booth.

5) The Willard couple's reception had a wedding caked shaped like an anchor and a potato salad shaped like a mermaid.

6) The Traut couple got married at the cemetery.

	sailor	undertaker	jockey	sanitation worker	audiologist	burglar
Henderson						
Madden						
Simon						
Shaw						
Willard						
Traut						

48.

Unusual Wedding Puzzle #2

Six couples (Dyer, Dorsey, Fleming, O'Neil, Patterson and Amato) got married one weekend. They each based the theme of their wedding and reception on their profession: cocktail pianist, yoga instructor, karate instructor, astronomer, pirate and speech therapist. Read the clues below and find out the theme of each couple's wedding.

1) The Dyer couple got married during a lunar eclipse.

2) The Dorsey couple wore a black belt at their wedding ceremony.

3) The Fleming couple got married at the National Stuttering Convention.

4) The O'Neil couple got married sitting in the lotus position.

5) The Patterson couple got married in a lounge.

6) During their ceremony, the Amato couple said, "AAARRRGH!" instead of, "I do."

	cocktail pianist	yoga instructor	karate instructor	astronomer	pirate	speech therapist
Dyer						
Dorsey						
Fleming						
O'Neil						
Patterson						
Amato						

49.

Unusual Weddings Puzzle #3

Six couples (Abbott, Walsh, Locke, Jacobs, Martin and Gardner) got married one weekend. They each based the theme of their wedding and reception on their profession, personal life or favorite place: professional gambler, twins, pickpocket, forest ranger, professional golfer and Disneyworld. Read the clues below to find out the theme of each couple's wedding.

1) The Abbott couple had a double ring ceremony and two identical wedding cakes.

2) The Walsh couple got married in Las Vegas.

3) At the Locke couple's reception three people were missing a wallet by the end of the evening.

4) The Jacobs couple was married by Yogi the Bear.

5) The Martin couple was married at the 9th hole.

6) At the Gardner's wedding ceremony, Mickey Mouse was the best man.

	professional gambler	twins	pickpocket	forest ranger	professional golfer	Disneyworld
Abbott						
Walsh						
Locke						
Jacob						
Martin						
Gardner						

50.

Unusual Wedding Puzzle #4

Six couples (Hogan, Casey, Carroll, Pendleton, Hitchcock and Anderson) got married one weekend. They each based the theme of their wedding and reception on their profession or hobby: psychic, divorce lawyer, clown, alligator wrestler, sky-diver and scuba diver. Read the clues to find out the theme of each couple's wedding.

1)   The Hogan couple got married next to a swamp in Florida.

2) The Casey couple signed a prenuptial agreement before the ceremony.

3) The Carroll couple had their tarot cards read before the ceremony. They found out that their marriage was only going to last for six months so they cancelled the wedding.

4) The Pendleton couple got married on a coral reef.

5) The Hitchcock couple wore a red rubber nose during the ceremony and reception.

6) The Anderson couple jumped out of an airplane and got married at an altitude of 4,000 feet.

	psychic	divorce lawyer	clown	alligator wrestler	sky-diver	scuba diver
Hogan						
Casey						
Carroll						
Pendleton						
Hitchcock						
Anderson						

51.

Unusual Wedding Puzzle #5

Six couples (Gordon, Rafferty, Peterson, Dylan, Lloyd and Hoffman) got married one weekend. They each based the theme of their wedding and reception on their profession or hobby: cartoonist, chess expert, cowboy, farmer, firefighter and interior decorator.   Read the clues below to find out the theme of each couple's wedding.

1) The bride's gown was made of wallpaper at the Gordon's wedding.

2) At the Rafferty's wedding, the bride and groom shouted "Checkmate!" instead of saying, "I do."

3) At the Peterson's wedding, the bride slid down a pole instead of walking down the aisle.

4) Sponge Bob Square Pants was the best man at the Dylan wedding.

5) At the Lloyd wedding, the groom threw a lariat around the bride and shouted, "I do!"

6) They had sheep for bridesmaids and donkeys for ushers at the Hoffman wedding.

	cartoonist	chess expert	cowboy	farmer	firefighter	interior decorator
Gordon						
Rafferty						
Peterson						
Dylan						
Lloyd						
Hoffman						

52.

Unusual Wedding Puzzle #6

Six couples (Wayne, Hall, Lawson, Chisholm, Morrison and Grant) got married one weekend. They each based the theme of their wedding and reception on their profession: magician, oceanographer, toll collector, meteorologist, librarian, and goalie. Read the clues below to find out the theme of each wedding.

1) The Wayne's wedding ceremony took place at a rest stop on the Massachusetts Turnpike.

2) The Hall's got married on a sunny day.

3) At the Lawson wedding, the groom accidentally made the bride disappear.

4) At the Chisholm wedding, the guests were all required to show their library card before they were allowed to enter the church.

5) At the Morrison's reception, there was a potato salad shaped like a dolphin and a wedding cake shaped like an octopus.

6) The groom wore a hockey mask at the Grant's wedding.

	magician	oceanographer	toll collector	meteorologist	librarian	goalie
Wayne						
Hall						
Lawson						
Chisholm						
Morrison						
Grant						

53.

Wedding Disaster Puzzle

Six brides have been friends since college (Marisa, Christina, Colleen, Victoria, Penelope and Rebecca). They all got married on the same weekend. Unfortunately, each wedding had something go wrong: the caterer, the mother-in-law, the honeymoon, the flowers, the limo driver and the tuxedos. When they got back from their honeymoon, they decided to go out to dinner and talk about their weddings. Read the clues below to find out what disaster happened at each of the friends' wedding.

1) Marisa said, "You should have seen the ushers at my wedding. They looked like a stuffed eggplant! You never saw such a ghastly color purple!"

2) Christina responded, "It couldn't have been as bad as my wedding. The mother of the groom stood up to make a toast and said, "Why couldn't my son have married that nice girl he dated in high school?"

3) Colleen snorted, "You haven't heard anything yet. At my wedding the florist mixed up my order with the funeral parlor down the street!"

4) Victoria said, "Listen to this one. Our limo driver didn't speak English and so he brought us to the wrong airport. We missed our flight and had to sleep overnight at Gate 23."

5) Penelope replied, "That's awful all right. But at least you had a nice honeymoon. Greg and I flew to Hawaii where it rained for the first week. When the sun came finally came out, a volcano erupted unexpectedly and we all had to be evacuated!"

6) Rebecca stated, "I'm so sorry to hear that. I guess I don't feel so bad about my reception now that I hear your stories. But the Beef Wellington did taste like an old boot!"

	caterer	honeymoon	limo driver	tuxedos	flowers	mother-in-law
Marisa						
Christina						
Colleen						
Victoria						
Penelope						
Rebecca						

54.

Maternity Ward Puzzle

Tuesday night was very busy on the maternity ward at Lakeview Hospital. Six babies were born between 6:00 PM and midnight (baby girl Marie- 7 lbs, 2 oz, baby girl Laura- 6 lbs, 10 oz, baby girl Sonya- 8 lbs, 4 oz, baby boy William- 7 lbs, 6 oz, baby boy Jared- 9 lbs, 8 oz, and baby boy Luke-8 lbs, 3 oz. Read the clues below to find out which baby was born to each family: Finn, Walsh, Jacob, Bronstein, Carlin, and Shaw.

1) The Finn family did not have a girl.

2) The Walsh family did not have a boy.

3) The Bronstein family's baby weighed the most.

4) The Jacob family's baby name did not have one syllable.

5) The Walsh family's baby weighed one ounce more than the Carlin family's baby.

6) The Shaw family's baby was the smallest.

	Baby Marie – 7 lbs. 2 oz.	Baby Laura – 6 lbs. 10 oz.	Baby Sonya – 8 lbs. 4 oz.	Baby William – 7 lbs. 6 oz.	Baby Jared – 9 lbs. 8 oz.	Baby Luke – 8 lbs. 3 oz.
Finn						
Walsh						
Bronstein						
Jacob						
Carlin						
Shaw						

55.

Weird Baby Names Puzzle #1

It was another busy night on the maternity ward at Lakeview Hospital. Nine babies were born between 6:00 PM and midnight. Each couple (Gilmore, Pimentel, Jenkins, Katz, Weiner and Schneider) gave the baby a name based upon their favorite pastime or interest: auto racing, football, The 3 Stooges, cartoons, conservation and Halloween. Read the clues below to find out what each couple chose to name their baby as a reflection of their favorite pastime or interest.

1) The Gilmore couple named their baby 'Lugnut'.

2) The Pimentel couple named their baby 'Butterfinger'.

3) The Jenkins couple named their baby 'Sponge Bob Square Pants'.

4) The Katz couple named their baby 'Rainforest'.

5) The Weiner couple named their triplets 'Moe', 'Larry' and 'Curly'.

6) The Schneider couple named their baby 'Superbowl'.

	auto racing	football	3 Stooges	cartoons	conservation	Halloween
Gilmore						
Pimentel						
Jenkins						
Katz						
Weiner						
Schneider						

56.

Weird Baby Names Puzzle #2

It was another busy night on the maternity ward at Lakeview Hospital. Six babies were born between 6:00 PM and midnight. Each couple (Novak, Webb, O'Leary, Leonard, Cumberland and Maddox) gave the baby a name based upon their favorite pastime: fortune telling, astronomy, meditation, scuba diving, landscaping and math. Read the clues below to find out what each couple chose to name their baby as a reflection of their favorite pastime.

1) The Novak couple named their baby 'Flipper.'

2) The Webb couple named their baby 'Infinity.'

3) The O'Leary couple named their baby 'Destiny.'

4) The Leonard couple named their baby 'Milky Way.'

5) The Cumberland couple named their baby 'Tranquility.'

6) The Maddox couple named their baby 'Mulch.'

	fortune telling	astronomy	meditation	scuba diving	landscaping	math
Novak						
Webb						
O'Leary						
Leonard						
Cumberland						
Maddox						

57.

Weird Baby Names Puzzle #3

It was another busy night on the maternity ward at Lakeview Hospital. Six babies were born between 6:00 PM and midnight. Each couple (Elliott, Hawes, Scollins, Malone, Richards and Goodman) gave the baby a name based upon their favorite pastime: dog obedience training, jewelry making, beauty pageants, antique collecting, gourmet cooking and whale watching. Read the clues below to find out what each couple chose to name their baby as a reflection of their favorite pastime.

1) The Malone couple named their baby 'Blubber.'

2) The Richards couple named their baby 'Bisquit.'

3) The Hawes couple named their baby 'Topaz.'

4) The Elliott couple named their baby 'Mahogany.'

5) The Scollins couple named their baby 'Olive Oil."

6) The Goodman couple named their baby 'Tiara.'

	dog obedience training	jewelry making	beauty pageants	antique collecting	gourmet cooking	whale watching
Malone						
Richards						
Hawes						
Elliott						
Scollins						
Goodman						

58.

Weird Baby Names Puzzle #4

It was another busy night on the maternity ward at Lakeview Hospital. Six babies were born between 6:00 PM and midnight. Each couple (O'Brien, Jackson, Fuller, Taylor, Williams and Thornton) gave the baby a name based upon their favorite pastime or profession: Mexican food, library science, hummingbirds, embroidery, dentistry, and the beach. Read the clues below to find out what each couple chose to name their baby as a reflection of their favorite pastime or profession.

1) The O'Brien's named their baby 'Flossie'.

2) The Jackson's couldn't decide whether to name their baby 'Nectar' or 'Honeysuckle'.

3) The Fuller's named their baby 'Shelly.'

4) The Taylor's named their baby 'Dewey Decimal.'

5) The Williams' named their baby 'Enchilada'.

6) The Thornton's named their baby 'Thimbelina'.

	Mexican food	library science	hummingbirds	embroidery	dentistry	the beach
O'Brien						
Jackson						
Fuller						
Taylor						
Williams						
Thornton						

59.

Leroy's Rhyming Birthday Party Puzzle #1

Leroy loves words that rhyme. Every year for his birthday his parents choose six words from the same word family and take him to six different places to represent each rhyming word (knight, fight, appetite, satellite, flight and fright). Help Leroy celebrate his birthday. Read the clues below to find out the location they chose for each rhyming word.

1) The first place they went was a boxing competition.

2) The second place was a medieval museum.

3) The third place they visited was a haunted house.

4) The fourth place on the tour was the airport.

5) The fifth place they went was the space museum

6) The last place they went was a gourmet restaurant.

	knight	fight	appetite	satellite	flight	fright
First place						
Second place						
Third place						
Fourth place						
Fifth place						
Sixth place						

60.

Leroy's Rhyming Birthday Party Puzzle #2

Leroy loves words that rhyme. Every year for his birthday his parents choose six words from the same word family and take him to six different places to represent each rhyming word (shark, bark, dark, park, spark, and aardvark). Help Leroy celebrate his birthday.   Read the clues below to find out the location they chose for each rhyming word.

1) The first place they took Leroy was the spooky house.

2) The second place they went was the zoo.

3) The third place they went was the playground.

4) The fourth place they went was a fireworks display.

5) For the fifth place they went to the aquarium.

6) The last place they went was the dog pound.

	shark	bark	dark	park	spark	aardvark
First Place						
Second Place						
Third Place						
Fourth place						
Fifth place						
Sixth place						

61.

Leroy's Rhyming Birthday Party Puzzle #3

Leroy loves words that rhyme. Every year for his birthday his parents choose six words from the same word family and take him to six different places to represent each rhyming word (spine, dine, sunshine, swine, Madeline and whine). Help Leroy celebrate his birthday. Read the clues below to find out the location they chose for each rhyming word.

1) The first place they went for Leroy's birthday was the beach.

2) The second place they went was a pig farm.

3) The third place they went was the children's library.

4) The fourth place they went was a daycare center.

5) The fifth place they went to visit was a chiropractor.

6) The last place they went was a gourmet restaurant.

	spine	dine	sunshine	swine	Madeline	whine
First place						
Second place						
Third place						
Fourth place						
Fifth place						
Sixth place						

62.

Leroy's Rhyming Birthday Party Puzzle #4

Leroy loves words that rhyme. Every year for his birthday his parents choose six words from the same word family and take him to six different places to represent each rhyming word (blend, trend, spend, lend, bend, and mend). Help Leroy celebrate his birthday.   Read the clues below to find out the location they chose for each rhyming word.

1) The first place they went to celebrate Leroy's birthday was the mall.

2) The second place they went was a fashion show.

3) The third place they went was an aerobics class.

4) The fourth place they went to visit was a seamstress shop.

5) The fifth place they went was a bank.

6) At the last place they went, they bought Leroy a smoothie.

	blend	trend	spend	lend	bend	mend
First place						
Second place						
Third place						
Fourth place						
Fifth place						
Sixth place						

63.

Leroy's Rhyming Birthday Party Puzzle #5

Leroy loves words that rhyme. Every year for his birthday his parents choose six words from the same word family and take him to six different places to represent each rhyming word (bell, carousel, tell, caramel, barbell, and cell). Help Leroy celebrate his birthday. Read the clues below to find out the location they chose for each rhyming word.

1) The first place they went to celebrate Leroy's birthday was the story hour at the library.

2) The second place they went was the candy store.

3) The third place they went was the local prison.

4) The fourth stop they made was the carnival.

5) At the fifth place, they climbed up inside a church steeple.

6) The last place they visited was a gym.

	bell	carousel	tell	caramel	barbell	cell
First place						
Second place						
Third place						
Fourth place						
Fifth place						
Sixth place						

64.

Leroy's Rhyming Birthday Party Puzzle #6

Leroy loves words that rhyme. Every year for his birthday his parents choose six words from the same word family and take him to six different places to represent each rhyming word (thrill, gill, drill, grill, dill, and chill). Help Leroy celebrate his birthday. Read the clues below to find out the location they chose for each rhyming word.

1) The first place they went to celebrate Leroy's birthday was an ice cube factory.

2) The second place they went was an oil rig.

3) At the third place they visited, they rode on a roller coaster.

4) The fourth place they visited was a pickle factory.

5) The fifth place they visited was the aquarium.

6) To finish the party, they went to a delicious barbecue.

	thrill	gill	drill	grill	dill	chill
First place						
Second place						
Third place						
Fourth place						
Fifth place						
Sixth place						

65.

Leroy's Rhyming Birthday Party Puzzle #7

Leroy loves words that rhyme. Every year for his birthday his parents choose six words from the same word family and take him to six different places to represent each rhyming word (drink, sink, shrink, stink, think and pink). Help Leroy celebrate his birthday.   Read the clues below to find out the location they chose for each rhyming word.

1) The first place they took Leroy for his birthday was a spelling bee.

2) The second place on the tour was a baby girl shower.

3) The third stop was a pig farm.

4) After that, they all felt a need to go to a juice bar.

5) Feeling refreshed, they went to a movie called, *"Honey, I Shrunk the Kids!"*

6) The last place they visited was a museum about the Titanic.

	drink	sink	shrink	stink	think	pink
First place						
Second place						
Third place						
Fourth place						
Fifth place						
Sixth place						

66.

Leroy's Rhyming Birthday Puzzle #8

Leroy loves words that rhyme. Every year for his birthday his parents choose six words from the same word family and take him to six different places to represent each rhyming word (vote, antidote, throat, moat, afloat and remote). Help Leroy celebrate his birthday. Read the clues below to find out the location they chose for each rhyming word.

1) The first place they took Leroy for his birthday was a medieval castle.

2) At the second stop on the tour, Leroy admired his uncle's new big screen TV.

3) The third place they visited was a poison control center.

4) For the fourth place they went on a tour of an air craft carrier.

5) The fifth place they took Leroy was a local election at the high school gym.

6) The last place Leroy enjoyed for his birthday was a sword swallowing competition.

	vote	antidote	throat	moat	afloat	remote
First place						
Second place						
Third place						
Fourth place						
Fifth place						
Sixth place						

67.

Leroy's Rhyming Birthday Party Puzzle #9

Leroy loves words that rhyme. Every year for his birthday his parents choose six words from the same word family and take him to six different places to represent each rhyming word (mice, sacrifice, spice, nice, rice, and dice). Help Leroy celebrate his birthday. Read the clues below to find out the location they chose for each rhyming word.

1) The first place they took Leroy to celebrate his birthday was a gourmet cooking store.

2) The second place they visited was a local newspaper to meet the etiquette expert.

3) For the third stop on the tour they visited the military troops at a nearby base.

4) The fourth place they enjoyed was a fancy casino.

5) The fifth place turned out to be the local pet store.

6) At the end of their tour, they had a lovely dinner at a Chinese restaurant.

	mice	sacrifice	spice	nice	rice	dice
First place						
Second place						
Third place						
Fourth place						
Fifth place						
Sixth place						

68.

Leroy's Rhyming Birthday Party Puzzle #10

Leroy loves words that rhyme. Every year for his birthday his parents choose six words from the same word family and take him to six different places to represent each rhyming word (splash, rash, crash, mash, trash and eyelash). Help Leroy celebrate his birthday. Read the clues below to find out the location they chose for each rhyming word.

1) The first place they took Leroy to celebrate his birthday was a potato processing plant.

2) The second place on the tour was the town dump.

3) The third place they stopped was a poison ivy patch.

4) The fourth place turned out to be a tour of a mascara factory.

5) The fifth place they enjoyed was a demolition derby.

6) The last stop they made was the beach.

	splash	rash	crash	mash	trash	eyelash
First place						
Second place						
Third place						
Fourth place						
Fifth place						
Sixth place						

69.

Las Vegas Disaster Puzzle #1

Six friends (Angie, Megan, Colleen, Zachary, Jonathan and Nathan) flew to Las Vegas for a weekend getaway. Unfortunately, they each experienced a disaster while they were there: lost luggage, food poisoning, stolen wallet, severe sunburn, rude taxi driver and got lost in the city.   Read the clues below to find out what terrible thing happened to them.

1)   Nathan couldn't change his clothes for two days.

2) Megan fell asleep by the pool.

3) Colleen left no tip.

4) Jonathan used his GPS to solve his problem.

5) Angie was sick in bed the whole weekend.

6)   Zachary reached into his pocket to pay for some poker chips; it was empty.

	lost luggage	food poisoning	stolen wallet	severe sunburn	rude taxi driver	lost in the city
Angie						
Megan						
Colleen						
Zachary						
Jonathan						
Nathan						

70.

Las Vegas Disaster Puzzle #2

Six friends (Hannah, Mae, Tianna, Thomas, Jack and Antonio) flew to Las Vegas for a weekend getaway. Unfortunately, they each experienced a disaster while they were there: stuck in elevator, sandstorm, power outage in the hotel, rude waitress, lost $5,000 at the Blackjack tables, and smoked a bad cigar. Read the clues below to find out what terrible thing happened to them.

1)   Tianna waited two hours to be rescued by the fire department.

2) Mae couldn't use her electric hair dryer the first morning.

3) Jack turned green.

4) Thomas wished he had a camel when he couldn't get a cab.

5) Hannah left no tip.

6) Antonio's wife refused to speak to him on the flight home.

	stuck in elevator	sandstorm	power outage	rude waitress	lost $5,000 gambling	smoked a bad cigar
Hannah						
Mae						
Tianna						
Thomas						
Jack						
Antonio						

Appendix A

ANSWER KEY

1. Favorite Game
- Billy – hide and seek
- Johnny – Candyland
- Mary – Go Fish
- Sally – hopscotch
- Jimmy – checkers
- Harry – Monopoly

2. Favorite Shape
- Billy – oval
- Jimmy – rectangle
- Joey – square
- Sally – triangle
- Mary – octagon
- Jane – circle

3.Sundae Toppings
- Cindy – chopped walnuts
- Billy – whipped cream
- Sally – hot fudge
- Jimmy – marshmallow
- Timmy – cherry
- Sarah – chocolate sprinkles

4. Omelettes
- Mr. Henshaw – spinach
- Mrs. Henshaw – broccoli
- Bill – ham
- Jimmy – bacon
- Joe – steak
- Cindy – onion

5. Slumber Party
- Melinda – 9:30 PM
- Ashleigh – went home
- Amy – 12:45 AM
- Kayla – 11:00 PM
- Lindsay – 2:30 AM
- Julia – 12:00

6. Burping Contest
- Joe – 18 burps
- Billy – 0 burps
- Harry – 10 burps
- Steve – 1 burp
- John – 9 burps
- Jake – 5 burps

7. Babysitter in Tears
- Davie – climbed up the chimney
- Wendy – put a newspaper in the dryer
- Jenny – decorated the dog
- Jimmy – hid the cell phone
- Shelly – put salt in the sugar bowl
- Tom – shaved the cat

8. Shirley's Blind Dates #1
- John – Monday
- Joe – Sunday
- Billy – Friday
- Harry – Tuesday
- Neal – Thursday
- Steve – Wednesday

9.Shirley's Blind Dates #2
- Bill – chronically late
- Phil – conceited
- Lanndon – boring
- Nathan – klutzy
- Edward – rude
- Jeffrey – cheap

10. Shirley's Blind Dates #3
- Sunday – chef
- Monday – pitcher
- Tuesday – lifeguard
- Wednesday – goalie
- Thursday – firefighter
- Friday – waiter

11. Diet Contest
- Betty – lost 8 lbs.
- Judy – lost 4 lbs.
- Phyllis – lost 3 lbs.
- Sylvia – gained 5 lbs.
- Jennifer – lost 15 lbs.
- Alyssa – lost 11 lbs.

12. **Hot Dog Eating Contest**
   - John – ate 18 hot dogs
   - Joe – ate 7 hot dogs
   - George – ate 14 hot dogs
   - Billy – ate 3 hot dogs
   - Harry – age 12 hot dogs
   - Same – age 13 hot dogs

13. **Restaurant**
   - Joe – spaghetti and meatballs
   - Virginia – eggplant parmesan
   - Melissa – salad
   - Bill – baked haddock
   - John – chowder
   - Susan – burger and fries

14. **Disasters**
   - Todd – tornado
   - Jill – blizzard
   - Bill – fire
   - Mary – hurricane
   - John – earthquake
   - Fred – flood

15. **Psychic**
   - Sue – invented weight loss pill
   - Mary – had 4 husbands
   - Jill – invented a potato masher
   - Penny – solved global warming
   - Cathy – abducted by aliens
   - Nancy – cure for bad breath

16. **Food Fight**
   - Jeremy – ketchup
   - Jill – grapes
   - Jenny – doughnut
   - Mary – whipped cream
   - Ethan – banana cream pie
   - Baby Tom – baby food

17. **School Nurse**
   - Bill – difficulty hearing
   - Mary – head lice
   - Joe – fell in a puddle
   - Jill – headache
   - Johnny – splinter
   - Sue – homesick

18. **Halloween Costume**
   - Jill – princess
   - Joe – ghost
   - Mary – bat
   - Penny – bride
   - John – Hulk
   - Bill – Ironman

19. **Commuting to Work**
   - Carl – train
   - Justin – car
   - Tex – horse
   - Luke – limo
   - Ahmed – camel
   - Nathan- on foot

20. **Treats at Circus**
   - Bill – t-shirt
   - Sally – stuffed animal
   - Mary – cotton candy
   - Tony – cotton candy
   - Benjamin – wax lips
   - George – peanuts

21. **Dog Tricks**
   - Ralph – play volleyball
   - Topper – knit a sweater
   - Boomer – sell lemonade
   - Bailey – mow the lawn
   - Skittles – guess your age
   - T-bone – fold the laundry

22. **Unusual Hair Color**
   - Monday – hot pink
   - Tuesday – green
   - Wednesday – black and white
   - Thursday – brown
   - Friday – red
   - Saturday – purple

23. **Unusual Diet**
   - Monday – bananas
   - Tuesday – salad
   - Wednesday – popcorn
   - Thursday – milk shake
   - Friday – cotton candy
   - Saturday – peanuts

24. **Places to Sleep**
   - Tommy – sleeping bag
   - Ginny – cradle
   - Sally – cot
   - Johnny – couch
   - Billy – bunk bed
   - Melissa – hotel

25. **Horse's Birthday Party**
   - First – carrots
   - Second – blanket
   - Third – bucket
   - Fourth – saddle
   - Fifth – bridle
   - Sixth – trailer

26. **Emotions**
> Mr. .Doherty – angry
> Jill – embarrassed
> Steve – proud
> George – starving
> Jessica – lazy
> Alyssa – jealous

27. **Stuffed Animals**
> First – anteater
> Second – camel
> Third – iguana
> Fourth – turtle
> Fifth – raccoon
> Sixth – kangaroo

28. **Rainy Day**
> Billy – pretend play
> Jane – jump rope
> John – drawing
> Mary – bake cookies
> Little Joey – hide and seek
> Jennifer – write poetry

29. **Favorite Food**
> Stephanie – watermelon
> Marta – brownies
> Lanndon – hot dog
> Melissa – cotton candy
> Christopher – pancakes
> Sarah – French fries

30. **Star-gazing**
> Mae – Milky Way
> Sarah – Big Dipper
> Travis – a cloud
> Lucy – an alien
> Noah – a comet
> Eric – Saturn

31. **Favorite Sounds**
> Abigail – purring
> James – creaking
> Jennifer – crackling
> Amanda – sizzling
> William – squealing
> Jonathan – rumbling

32. **Hide and Seek**
> Peter – under the bed
> James – on the back porch
> Marisa – in the chandelier
> Linda – in the fireplace
> William – in the dog's crate
> Susie – behind the couch

33. **Good Samaritan**
> Jerry – raking leaves
> Bill – shoveling snow
> Jill – driving a neighbor
> Jessica – charity car wash
> Dan – working at an animal shelter
> Belinda – rescued a cat from a tree

34. **Bad Boss**
> Monday – secretary
> Tuesday – shipping department
> Wednesday – accountant
> Thursday – salesman
> Friday – custodian
> Saturday – limo driver

35. **What a Nightmare**
> Monday – got lost in a strange city
> Tuesday – threatened by a growling dog
> Wednesday – drowned in maple syrup
> Thursday – swept up by a tornado
> Friday - died
> Saturday – inherited a skink farm

36. **Life of Crime**
> George – grand theft auto
> Sam - forgery
> Bob – illegal gambling
> Owen - counterfeiting
> Nathan – bank robbery
> Phil – shop lifting

37. **Accident Prone Son**
> Monday – burnt eyelashes
> Tuesday – fell off a cliff
> Wednesday – concussion
> Thursday – black eye
> Friday – poison ivy
> Saturday – poison mushrooms

38. **Mixed-up Suitcases**
> Psychic – got the snake charmer's suitcase
> Jeweler – got the hippie's suitcase
> Snake Charmer – got psychic's suitcase
> Body Builder – got the beauty queen's suitcase
> Hippie – got the jeweler's suitcase
> Beauty queen – got the body builder's suitcase

39. **Car That Was a Lemon**
> Monday – muffler fell off
> Tuesday – flat tire
> Wednesday – hole in the gas tank
> Thursday – broken windshield wipers
> Friday – broken horn
> Saturday – broken speedometer

40. **Very Rude Daughter #1**
    Brandon – his car
    Gregory – his weight
    Matthew – hit baldness
    Rob – his crooked teeth
    Adam – his education
    Christopher – his clothes

41. **Very Rude Daughter #2**
    Charles – his physique
    Jim – his IQ
    Phil – his cologne
    Ben – his class ring
    Sergio – his tie
    George – his buck teeth

42. **Very Rude Daughter #3**
    Nathan – short
    Jack – his yellow teeth
    Jeremy – his ears
    Lennie – his nose
    Mario – his conversational skills
    Sam – condo

43. **Very Rude Daughter #4**
    Bart – his paunch
    Sam – his looks
    Jeremy – his table manners
    Jack – his cell phone
    Steve – his artwork
    Bill – his double chin

44. **Little Billy's Revenge**
    Olivia – thimble
    Mark – super glue
    Lauren – potato chips
    Peter – toothpaste
    Ben – pebble
    Robin – frog

45. **Todd's Aliens**
    January – air conditioner
    February – thimble
    March – mirror
    April – ladder
    May – puppy
    June – hair elastics

46. **Joe's Exotic Careers**
    First – dolphin trainer
    Second – sumo wrestler
    Third – trapeze artist
    Fourth – alligator wrestler
    Fifth – sword swallower
    Sixth – snake charmer

47. **Unusual Wedding #1**
    Henderson – jockey
    Madden – sanitation worker
    Simon – burglar
    Shaw – audiologist
    Willard – sailor
    Traut – undertaker

48. **Unusual Wedding #2**
    Dyer – astronomer
    Dorsey – karate instructor
    Fleming – speech therapist
    O'Neil – yoga instructor
    Patterson – cocktail pianist
    Amato – pirate

49. **Unusual Wedding #3**
    Abbott – twins
    Walsh – professional gambler
    Locke – pickpocket
    Jacob – forest ranger
    Martin – professional golfer
    Gardner – Disneyworld

50. **Unusual Wedding #4**
    Hogan – alligator wrestler
    Casey – divorce lawyer
    Carroll – psychic
    Pendleton – scuba diving
    Hitchcock – clown
    Anderson – sky diver

51. **Unusual Wedding #5**
    Gordon – interior decorator
    Rafferty – chess expert
    Peterson – firefighter
    Dylan – cartoonist
    Lloyd – cowboy
    Hoffman – farmer

52. **Unusual Wedding #6**
    Wayne – toll collector
    Hall – meteorologist
    Lawson – magician
    Chisholm – librarian
    Morrison – oceanographer
    Grant – goalie

53. **Wedding Disaster**
    Marisa – tuxedoes
    Christina – mother-in-law
    Colleen – flowers
    Victoria – limo driver
    Penelope – honeymoon
    Rebecca – caterer

54. **Maternity Ward**
   Finn – William, 7 lbs., 6 oz.
   Walsh – Sonya, 8 lbs. 4 oz.
   Jacob – Marie, 7 lbs. 2 oz.
   Bronstein – Jared, 9 lbs., 8 oz.
   Carlin – Luke, 8 lbs., 3 oz.
   Shaw – Laura, 6 lbs., 10 oz.

55. **Weird Baby Names #1**
   Gilmore – auto racing
   Pimentel – Halloween
   Jenkins – cartoons
   Katz – conservation
   Weiner – Three Stooges
   Schneider – football

56. **Weird Baby Names #2**
   Novak – scuba diving
   Webb – math
   O'Leary – fortune telling
   Leonard – astronomy
   Cumberland – meditation
   Maddox – landscaping

57. **Weird Baby Names #3**
   Elliott – antique collecting
   Hawes – jewelry making
   Scollins – gourmet cooking
   Malone – whale watching
   Richards – dog obedience
   Goodman – beauty pageants

58. **Weird Baby Names #4**
   O'Brien – dentist
   Jackson – hummingbirds
   Fuller – the beach
   Taylor – librarian
   Williams – Mexican food
   Thornton – embroidery

59. **Leroy's Rhyming Birthday Party #1**
   1st – fight
   2nd – knight
   3rd – fright
   4th – flight
   5th – satellite
   6th – appetite

60. **Leroy's Rhyming Birthday Party #2**
   1st – dark
   2nd – aardvark
   3rd – park
   4th – spark
   5th – shark
   6th – bark

61. **Leroy's Rhyming Birthday Party #3**
   1st – sunshine
   2nd – swine
   3rd – Madeline
   4th – whine
   5th – spine
   6th – dine

62. **Leroy's Rhyming Birthday Party #4**
   1st – spend
   2nd – trend
   3rd – bend
   4th – mend
   5th – lend
   6th – blend

63. **Leroy's Rhyming Birthday Party #5**
   1st – tell
   2nd – caramel
   3rd – cell
   4th – carousel
   5th – bell
   6th – barbell

64. **Leroy's Rhyming Birthday Party #6**
   1st – chill
   2nd – drill
   3rd – thrill
   4th – dill
   5th – gill
   6th – grill

65. **Leroy's Rhyming Birthday Party #7**
   1st – think
   2nd – pink
   3rd – stink
   4th – drink
   5th – shrink
   6th – sink

66. **Leroy's Rhyming Birthday Party #8**
   1st – moat
   2nd – remote
   3rd – antidote
   4th – afloat
   5th – vote
   6th – throat

67. **Leroy's Rhyming Birthday Party #9**
   1st spice
   2nd – nice
   3rd – sacrifice
   4th – dice
   5th – mice

6th – rice

68. **Leroy's Rhyming Birthday Party #10**
    1st – mash
    2nd – trash
    3rd – rash
    4th – crash
    5th – crash
    6th – splash

69. **Las Vegas Disaster #1**
    Angie – food poisoning
    Megan – bad sunburn
    Colleen – rude taxi driver
    Zachary – stolen wallet
    Jonathan – got lost in the city
    Nathan – lost luggage

70. **Las Vegas Disaster #2**
    Tianna – stuck in an elevator
    Mae – power outage
    Jack – smoked a bad cigar
    Thomas – sandstorm
    Hannah – rude waitress
    Antonio – lost money at Blackjack

www.ingramcontent.com/pod-product-compliance
Lightning Source LLC
Chambersburg PA
CBHW080447030726
47592CB00011B/3015